the world according to

julius

the world according to
julius

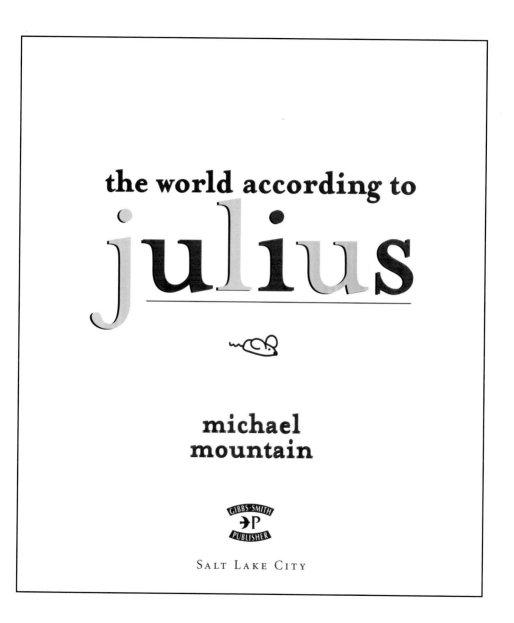

michael
mountain

GIBBS·SMITH
→P
PUBLISHER

SALT LAKE CITY

First Edition

05 04 03 02 01 5 4 3 2

Text copyright © 2001 by Michael Mountain

Photographic copyright © 2001 by Jana de Peyer, Willie Green,
Chandra Forsythe, and Don Bruce.

Map of Kittyville copyright © 2001 Best Friends Animal Sanctuary

Published by
Gibbs Smith, Publisher
P.O. Box 667
Layton, UT 84041

Orders: (1-800) 748-5439
www.gibbs-smith.com

Designed by Dawn DeVries Sokol
Edited by Gail Yngve

Library of Congress Cataloging-in-Publication Data
Mountain, Michael.
The world according to Julius/Michael Mountain. —1st ed.
p. cm.
ISBN 1-58685-109-8
1. Cats—Utah—Kanab—Anecdotes. 2. Animal rescue—Utah—
Kanab—Anecdotes. 3. Best Friends Animal Sanctuary. I. Title.
SF445.5.M69 2001
636.80832'0979251—dc21
2001003406

contents

The TLC Cat Club
at Best Friends Animal Sanctuary

About seven hundred cats can be found at Best Friends on any given day. Many of them just need to spend a few weeks at the sanctuary before they're ready to go to good new homes. But about half of them make up what we call the TLC Cat Club — for cats like Julius who have special needs. These little guys come to us from shelters around the country because they've had trouble finding good homes. They may have had some physical or emotional trauma, or they're older or not so well and need special care and a little extra help getting around.

This book is about the TLC Cat Club. When we built Benton's House (their special home at the sanctuary), the conventional wisdom was still that cats like these were unadoptable because people would always prefer a lively healthy kitten to an older cat who needed a little extra help.

Over the years, this notion has been changing. Every day, letters pour in to the sanctuary from people who have adopted a special-needs cat or dog and have discovered the joy and depth of a new and wonderful relationship.

The essential facts of this story about the TLC cats are all true. The people who look after Julius and his pals had no doubt, for example, that he was becoming the "chair*purrson*" of the group. All I have done is recast the facts in a context that may or may not have been exactly what the cats were saying to each other.

But then, what cats *really* say to each other—and get people to do for them—might be too far beyond the bounds of accepted belief to be told in a book like this!

—*Michael Mountain*

Charmed
and Charming

At the dawn of the twenty-first century, nobody really thought that it would fall to a charming but slightly goofy cat to lead civilization into a new era.

Julius hardly seemed qualified for the role he was stepping into. Indeed, he was delightfully unaware that he *had* stepped into it. This sweet-tempered, cross-eyed orange cat couldn't even walk in a straight line, let alone take the reins of an ancient heritage, which is what he was about to do. Apart from anything else, he was neurologically impaired, which meant, among other things, that his back end was never going in the same direction as his front end.

An orphan because of his disability, Julius had never had a real home. He just moved from shelters to foster homes to more shelters. At each stop along the way, the people who cared for him despaired of ever being able to place him in a permanent home.

But Julius led a charmed life. Or maybe he just charmed everyone else's life. Either way, in a world that seemed more and more obsessed with going in straight lines, setting goals, and reaching destinations, Julius simply went wherever life took him. And, eventually, it took him to Best Friends Animal Sanctuary, where he was soon to become Chair*purrson* of the TLC Cat Club and usher in a new millennium.

Ancient
Heritage

The TLC Cat Club at Best Friends was not, of course, the first place where cats had gathered to shape the course of civilization. There had been TLC Cat Clubs throughout history, although people were not aware of most of them.

The most remarkable and successful club to date was in ancient Egypt. It had come about quite by chance. Cats began to gather in Egypt when word spread that there were many mice in people's homes and an excellent cat litter box just outside, known locally as the Sahara Desert.

It was, all in all, the perfect place for a cat sanctuary, and Julius's ancestors had made the most of it, building a feline-friendly civilization that would last thousands of years. There were pyramids to play in, temples to be deified in, and the best cat-protection laws anywhere. Indeed, in some parts of the country, it became a capital offense to kill a cat—even by accident.

Beauty, dignity, and good manners became the order of the day; the arts flourished, people behaved themselves, for the most part, and they even built elaborate boats to take cats into the afterlife when their time arrived.

Thousands of years later, ancient Egypt continued to be recognized as one of the greatest civilizations of history. But that was all a long time ago, and now, as another millennium drew to a close, cats were reporting in urgently from all over the world that it was time to convene a new TLC Cat Club. Once again, they said, civilization and culture were in decline. The situation was urgent. A new direction was needed.

The First
Chairpurrson

The founder of the new TLC Cat Club was Benton. He was an autocrat in the true ancient Egyptian tradition. As soon as he arrived at Best Friends Animal Sanctuary, he saw it as a perfect place to re-create the old empire. The local landscape, he pointed out to his associates, was not that different from their ancient home: a majestic red-rock canyon, white cliffs in the distance (just like the Valley of the Kings, near the Temples of Luxor and Karnak), a creek running through the canyon (not as wide as the Nile, but it would do), and a huge natural litter box stretching into the distance—for emergency use in the unlikely event that the weekly delivery truck was late.

Benton had come to Best Friends after being hit by a car. His family had moved to another town and left him behind—a very uncivilized thing to do. Never one to accept a situation that was less than entirely satisfactory, Benton had gone in search of them. A neighbor rescued him. "He was actually heading in the right direction," she said when she brought him to the sanctuary. "But then he tried to cross a busy street. . . ."

The accident left him with a broken paw, which he considered a badge of honor, proclaiming himself founder and Chair*purrson* of a new TLC Cat Club for the modern age—a home for cats with special disabilities.

Benton inspired the building of Benton's House, where the TLC cats would live. (There were murmurings that he had designed it to look a bit like an ancient cat temple.) Once the cats with special needs all moved in, the Chair*purrson* became something of an egomaniac. Not that anyone disputed his authority. He just waved his clubfoot around and cats and people all did what they were told.

Everybody, that is, except Julius. Not that the little new arrival was unwilling; he simply couldn't quite get it together to go exactly where he was told. Sometimes, he even bumped into Benton when Hizzoner was having his afternoon treats. This would normally have been considered a major "faux paw." But in Julius's case, even Benton didn't seem to mind.

For the next seven years, Hizzoner ruled the TLC Cat Club with an iron paw while carefully cultivating the image of a benevolent, cuddly patriarch by never missing a photo op with children.

But eventually, old Benton went over the Rainbow Bridge. Since the entire notion of a new world order, modeled on ancient Egypt, had been his, this left a real gap. Someone was going to have to take over as Chair*purrson* and finish the important work of leading civilization into a new era.

There were hundreds of cats to choose from in Benton's House: handsome cats and scruffy cats, show cats and street cats, and cats of every description—worldly, hypnotic, aloof, innocent, charismatic, everything. But no single cat could muster the unquestioned authority that Benton had always commanded.

In any case, these were different times. The new TLC Cat Club was not ancient Egypt, and it could no longer be run by a self-appointed cat deity. There was no way the cats would agree to another feline pharaoh. In this modern world, there would have to be elections.

A full-scale election campaign was launched, and several cats were nominated. To no one's surprise, Julius was not among the nominees.

The Campaign

Three-legged Blackjack could probably have hopped away with the election, if he had wanted it. He had been around as long as Benton and was as fast on three feet as most other cats on four.

Blackjack was accepted as the elder statesman of the clan, but he had a "been there, done that" attitude to politics and simply declined to run. Plus, he was far too wise to accept the nomination, even if it were handed to him in a bowl. The last thing he wanted was to trade in his revered elder-statesman status for the endless challenges of being a top cat.

Besides, in their new media-centric world, the cats needed a Chair*purrson* who was photogenic and telegenic.

Supporting Her Right to Bear Claws

If being "mediagenic" was that important, Camille was a very strong candidate. She was always on the A-list of the TV crews that were showing up in growing numbers at the TLC Cat Club.

But Camille took some unpopular positions—in particular, her position on being picked up. As a hard-liner, she defended her right *not* to be picked up, and she cited her Second Amendment right to bear arms, plus teeth and claws, when challenged by anyone who *tried* to pick her up.

Camille's candidacy fell apart one afternoon after she went overboard and staged a hostage drama when a visitor from New Jersey tried to pick her up.

"I was grooming some of the cats, and Camille climbed into my lap," Elaine, the visitor, explained later. "She seemed very happy, but when I tried to pick her up (which was simply so that I could put her down), she sank her claws into my leg."

Elaine tried negotiating her way out of the crisis but eventually had to call for a rescue team. In the standoff that followed, everyone agreed that Camille was not about to back down, so the negotiators brought in some adoption forms, which Elaine agreed to sign unconditionally. The following day, she took Camille back to New Jersey with her.

"I absolutely fell in love with her," Elaine reported later. "And she only bit me a few times!"

Everyone was relieved that Camille, now seen as a public-relations disaster, was off the ballot and out of the TLC Cat Club altogether.

The Health Care Candidate

Also on the A-list was Bijou, a stunningly handsome former show cat from ancient Egyptian stock, who had been hit by a car and then abandoned at the animal hospital when his people heard what the vet bills would be.

Bijou had been the darling of the health care lobby, but they began to cool on him when he said he didn't want to spend the rest of his life making TV commercials about incontinence.

The Knockout Candidate

Simon looked as though he would walk away with the female vote. Women agreed, right across the board, that this huge, gorgeous, fluffy cat was a knockout.

The trouble was that he actually *was* a knockout. A few days after he went to a new home, his bewildered family brought him back, explaining that he had attacked their huge St. Bernard dog. This episode added to Simon's mystique, but party officials were worried that there might be a backlash later on.

The New Chair*purrson*

In the heat of all the campaign rhetoric, the pundits and pollsters kept missing the simple fact that the most popular cat by far among people who came to visit the sanctuary was Julius.

Everybody who met him fell in love with this cross-eyed, slightly goofy, sweet-spirited, and utterly charming youngster who somehow captured the essence of what civilization really needed at the dawn of a new millennium. Blackjack seized the moment and made a speech nominating Julius for Chair*purrson*.

"We all know," he began by acknowledging to the other cats, "that Julius's elevator does not go all the way to the top, that he is not playing with a full deck, and that he's a brick short of a full load.

"But this is not ancient Egypt, and none of us here can run for office as the perfect feline deity. We are products of our own time—cast-offs and dropouts from a society that has become estranged from its own nature.

"And Julius is the new spirit that emerges from that wasteland—a spirit of innocence and simplicity that everyone is looking for in an era that is searching for new values."

As the three-legged elder statesman returned to his favorite perch up in the rafters, all eyes turned to the cross-eyed kitty who was just waking up from a nice snooze and getting ready for his favorite time of day: afternoon treats.

He was promptly proclaimed Chair*purrson* of the TLC Cat Club by a unanimous vote.

Where the Treats Are

One reason for Julius's great popularity was that he was a natural when it came to relating to people. He was always at the door to greet visitors, who were charmed and captivated by his zest for life as they watched him set off across the room in search of treats or whatever else took his fancy.

He also resisted any well-intentioned offer to pick him up and save him the effort of a long zigzag journey across the room.

The point, Julius seemed to be saying, was not to get from here to there in the shortest time. It was, rather, to set out across the room and see where you ended up. As it turned out, he always seemed to end up where the treats were.

This remarkable ability intrigued everyone who met him. Indeed, rumors soon began to circulate that the new Chair*purr*son was, in fact, a being of extraordinary depth and wisdom, whose every action held some profound significance.

Especially his journeys to the other side of the room.

Journey to the Other Side of the Room

Introduction
for students and seekers

Life is a journey, a great and wonderful journey to the other side of the room. If the only point were to get from one side of the room to the other as quickly as possible, who among us here at the TLC Cat Club would be winners? But life isn't just about where one is going. It's about how one gets there and what happens along the way. So now, let us follow Julius as we journey together to the other side of the room.

Start here at one side of the room. Who will we meet first?

. . . Well, look who it is: my best friend, Malcom . . .

. . . stop for some cuddles from a nice visitor . . .

*... check out
interesting
bucket of combs
and brushes
and stuff ...*

*... discuss
important
matters of state
with Funnyface
Patience ...*

. . . stop to be interviewed by Tomato the Cat, investigative reporter for Best Friends *magazine, on whether all life is a journey to the other side of the room . . .*

. . . bump into Thomas and wake him up from a nice snooze . . . excuse me, Thomas . . .

. . . discover excellent bowl of treats.

Across the Room

All Over the World

The first signs of success in terms of changing the course of civilization was when Julius became a pop icon and people everywhere wanted to embark on their own journeys to the other side of the room. Indeed, the entire world was soon caught up in a craze of journeying to the other side of the room.

Questions poured into the TLC Cat Club as to whether one's journey should be across the same room every day or whether one could sometimes journey to the other side of the road or, perhaps, to the other side of the office. (Orthodox journeyers pointed out that Julius always crossed the *same* room.)

Important philosophers lectured on how the journey was really an *inner* journey and that one should not expect to find a physical treat at the end so much as an *inner* treat.

Web sites offered e-journeys across e-rooms with e-treats.

A flourishing new Psychic Pets Network of animal communicators sprang up, offering help to uncertain journeyers and promising to deliver personalized messages, relayed directly from the Chair*purrson*.

Of course, the essence of Julius's journey to the other side of the room was that each day's expedition was different, interesting, and unique precisely because his back legs were never going in quite the same direction as his front legs. So the big question for others was: Can you actually have an authentic journey to the other side of the room if your legs are all going in the same direction? And can it ever be a legitimate journey if you only have two legs to start with?

The answer, as more and more people came to realize, was that the key to fulfillment lay not in trying to do the same thing as Julius, but in welcoming a cat like Julius into your home.

Soon after that—which was the true measure of Blackjack's wisdom—people were showing up at shelters across the country, asking to adopt a cat with some kind of special need or disability.

To prepare all these special-needs kitties for the sudden new interest in them, Patience, the Miss Manners of the TLC Cat Club, put together a brochure on how to greet people when they arrived at the local shelter. It was entitled *Julius's Guide to Welcoming Guests*.

Julius's Guide
to Welcoming Guests

Funnyface Patience says that being a social success isn't so much to do with the way you look. It's more about making your guests look and feel wonderful. That means you should always make your guests the center of attention.

If you're not sure what to say, like Virginia, don't get introverted. Just go up to visitors and ask them about themselves.

It's best not to argue in front of visitors over who gets to go to which home.

Instead, focus on what you do best, and let the details take care of themselves.

Always be as cute as you can be.

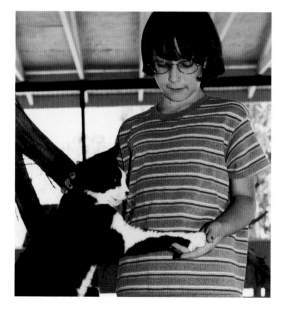

And if you're missing a paw, like Blackjack, don't draw attention to it. Just hold out the other one.

If you can't get around too well yourself, like Harriet, then ask your guests to give you a ride. They'll be happy to oblige.

You don't have to dress up or anything. Just keep a comb handy, like Malcom does, so your guests can help you look your best.

See? It's easy when you get the hang of it.

A New World

Sometime in the near future…

As *Julius's Guide to Welcoming Guests* reached the top of the best-seller lists, it was clear that the mission of the new TLC Cat Club was succeeding beyond Blackjack and Patience's wildest expectations. Civilization was once again taking a new course, as had happened in ancient Egypt when the first TLC Cat Club took the reins.

Specifically, cats with special needs, who until now had faced a dismal and very uncertain future in shelters, were now in enormous demand. Shelters could scarcely keep up with the requests to adopt them.

People who didn't have the time or the means to care for a special-needs cat or dog at home would care for their neighborhood alley cats or help out at the local shelter. As the new millennium progressed, kindness to animals became the new ethic.

This was all part of a general shift in people's priorities. Things like wealth, social status, being politically correct, and generally

keeping up with the Joneses became less important. Caring about the animals that lived around them—not just cats and dogs, but the wildlife and even the little bugs that flew in the window (not to mention other people, too!)—began to matter a lot more.

People also discovered that all this concern for the animals was not pure altruism: their own lives were suddenly a whole lot better, too. Nobody had realized it before, but so much of the anxiety and depression in people's lives stemmed from their feeling cut off from the natural world around them. Simply having a cat or dog to care for and care about made a huge difference in their own health and outlook.

Meanwhile, back at the TLC Cat Club, life soon settled down and continued pretty much as normal, except for the fact that there were, of course, far fewer cats needing to come to the sanctuary in the first place since so many were being adopted into new homes.

Patience continued to watch over Julius and make sure that he always ended up where the treats were—not that he needed much help doing that.

And Julius spent his time greeting visitors to the TLC Cat Club and enjoying his journeys to the other side of the room—blissfully unaware, apparently, that he and his kind had done so much to bring joy and contentment into the lives of the people who loved them.